TO:

FROM:

GRANDFATHERS
are the
BEST

Published by Sellers Publishing, Inc.
161 John Roberts Road, South Portland, ME 04106
Visit us at www.sellerspublishing.com • E-mail: rsp@rsvp.com

Copyright © 2018 Sellers Publishing, Inc.
All rights reserved.

Managing Editor: Mary L. Baldwin
Production Editor: Charlotte Cromwell
Cover and interior design by Charlotte Cromwell
Compiled by Charlotte Cromwell

ISBN-13: 978-1-4162-4639-8

No portion of this book may be reproduced or transmitted in any form, or by any means, electronic or mechanical, including photographing, recording, or by any information and storage retrieval system, without written permission from the publisher.

Printed and bound in China.

10 9 8 7 6 5 4 3 2 1

Image credits on page 64.

GRANDFATHERS are the BEST

great dads get promoted to grandfathers

SELLERS
PUBLISHING

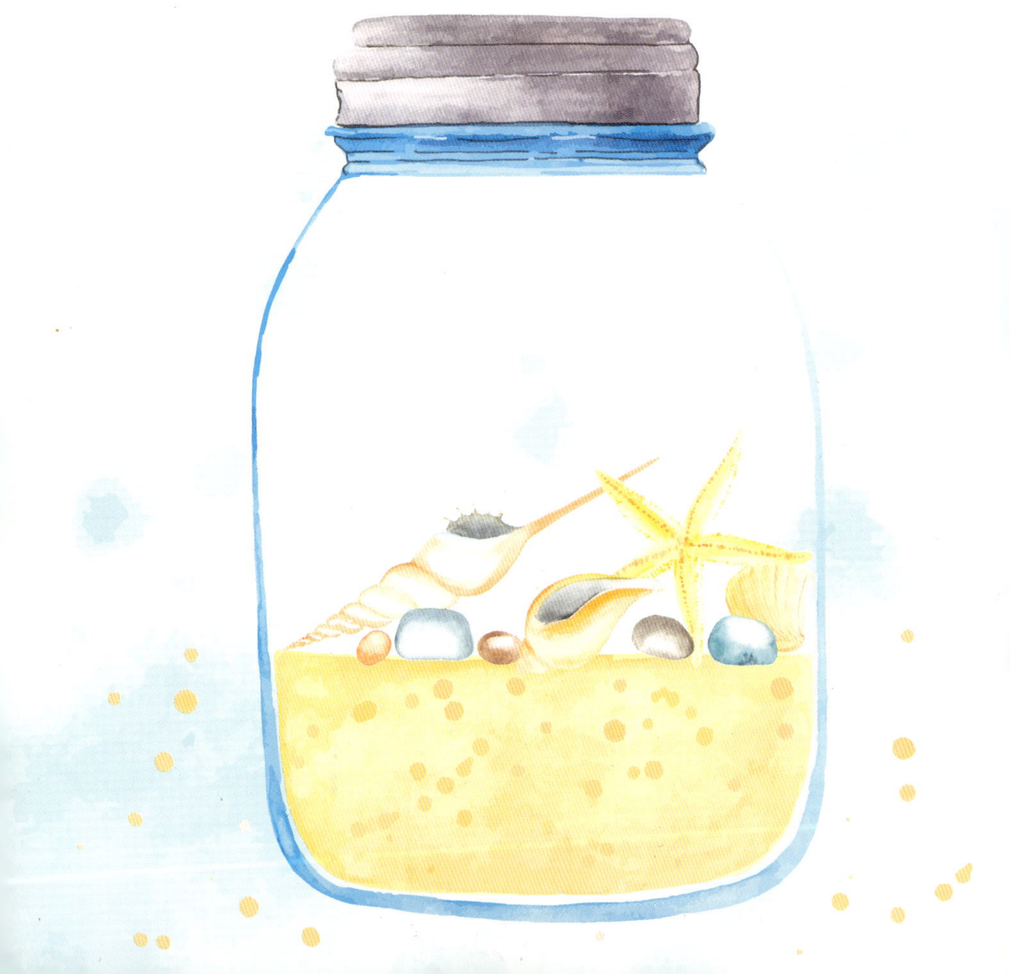

A GRANDFATHER
is someone with silver in his hair and gold in his heart.

Author Unknown

To a small child, the perfect granddad is unafraid of big dogs and fierce storms but absolutely terrified of the word *boo*.

Robert Brault

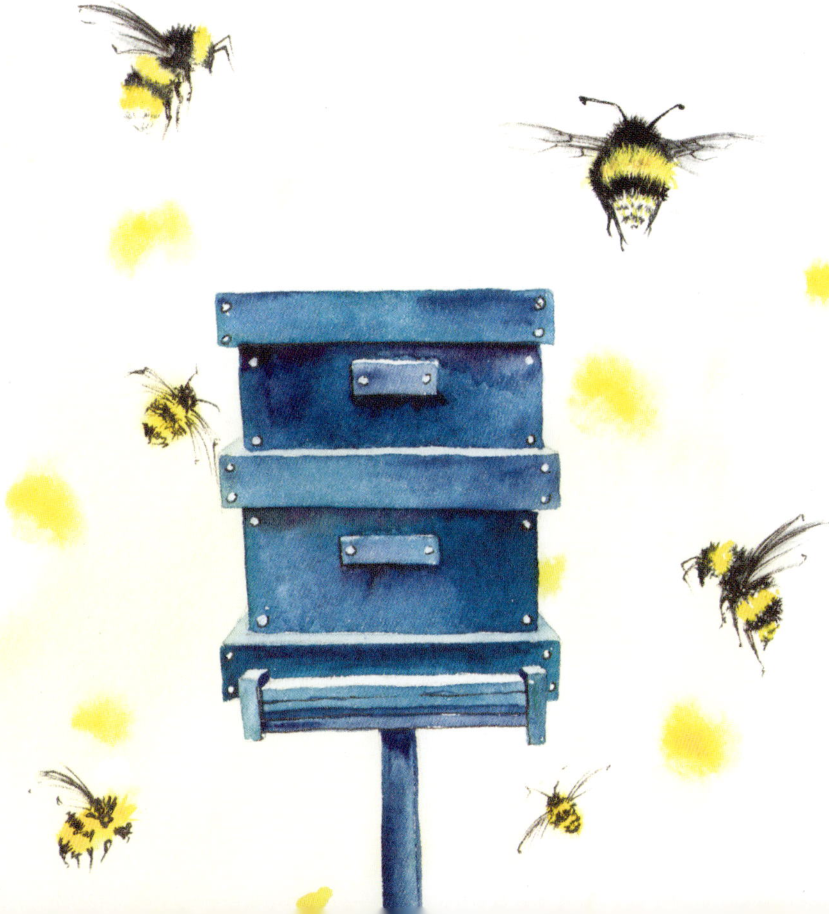

More and more,
when I single out the person
who inspired me most,

I go back to my grandfather.

James Earl Jones

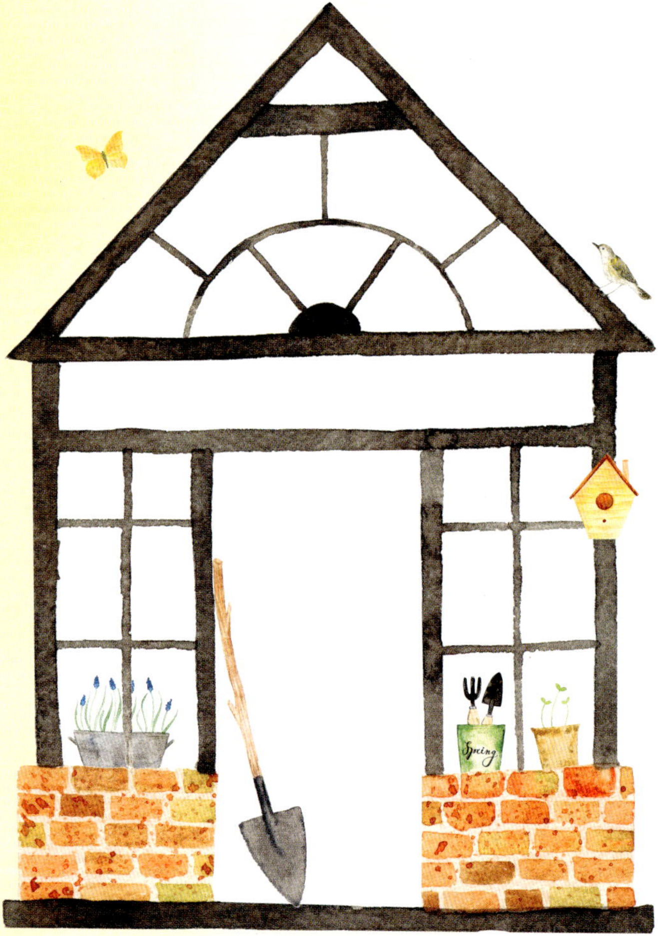
Spring

My **grandpa** taught me how to live off the land.

Hank Williams Jr

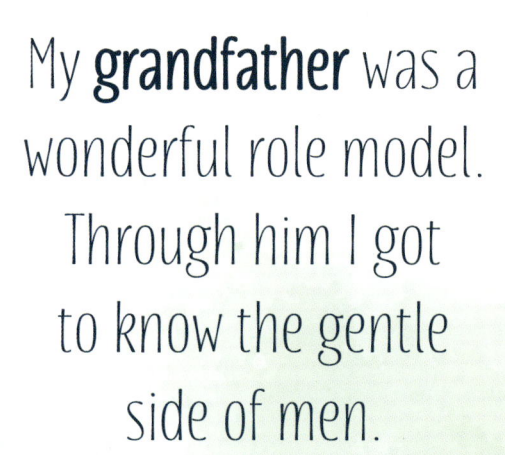

My **grandfather** was a wonderful role model. Through him I got to know the gentle side of men.

Sarah Long

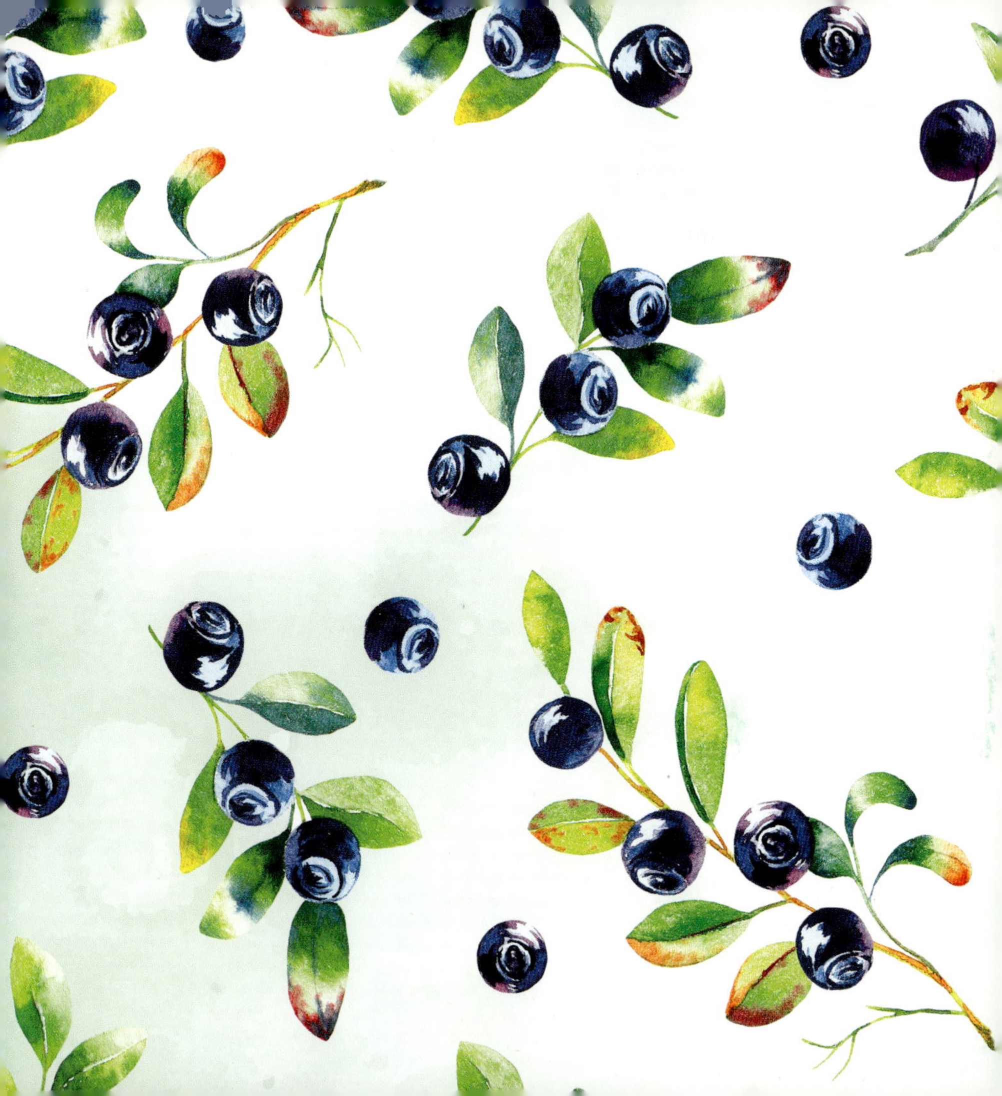

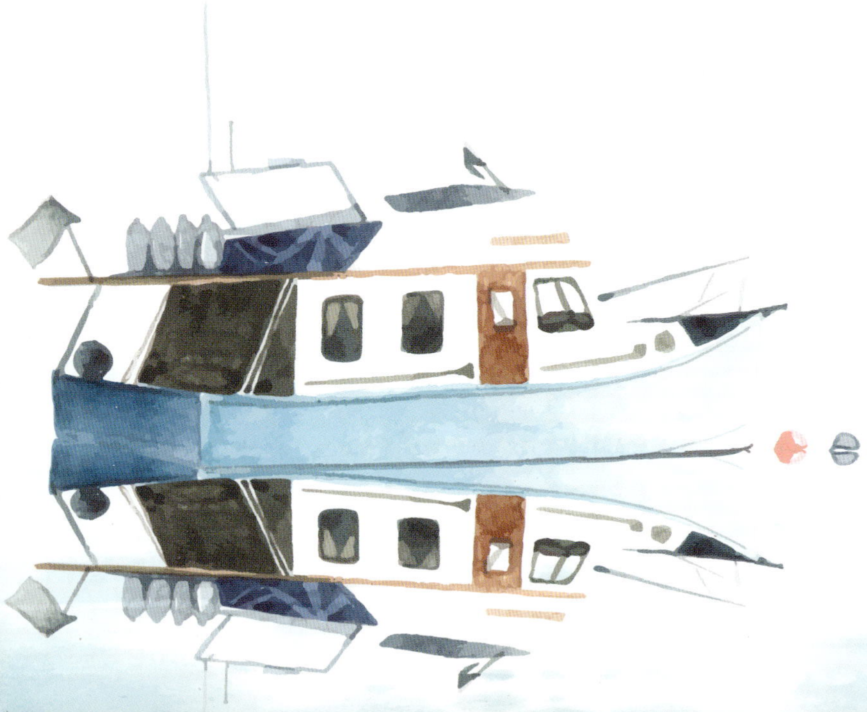

A child's eyes
light up when they
see their **Grandpa**.

Author Unknown

Grandfathers are for loving and fixing things.

Author Unknown

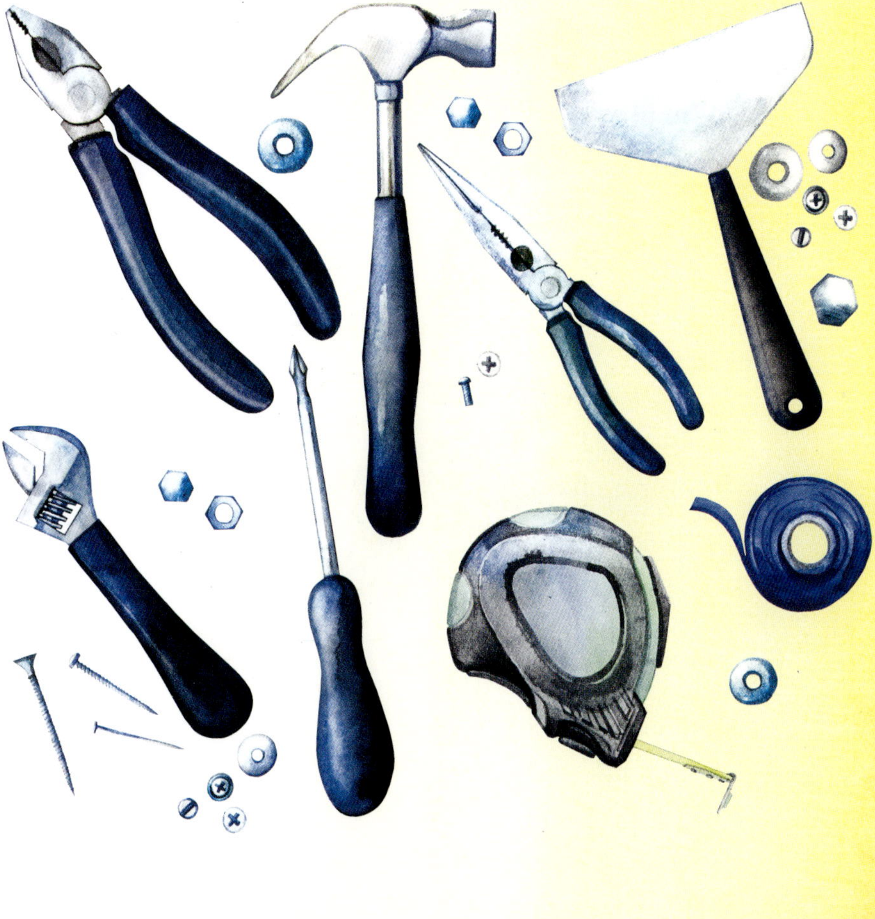

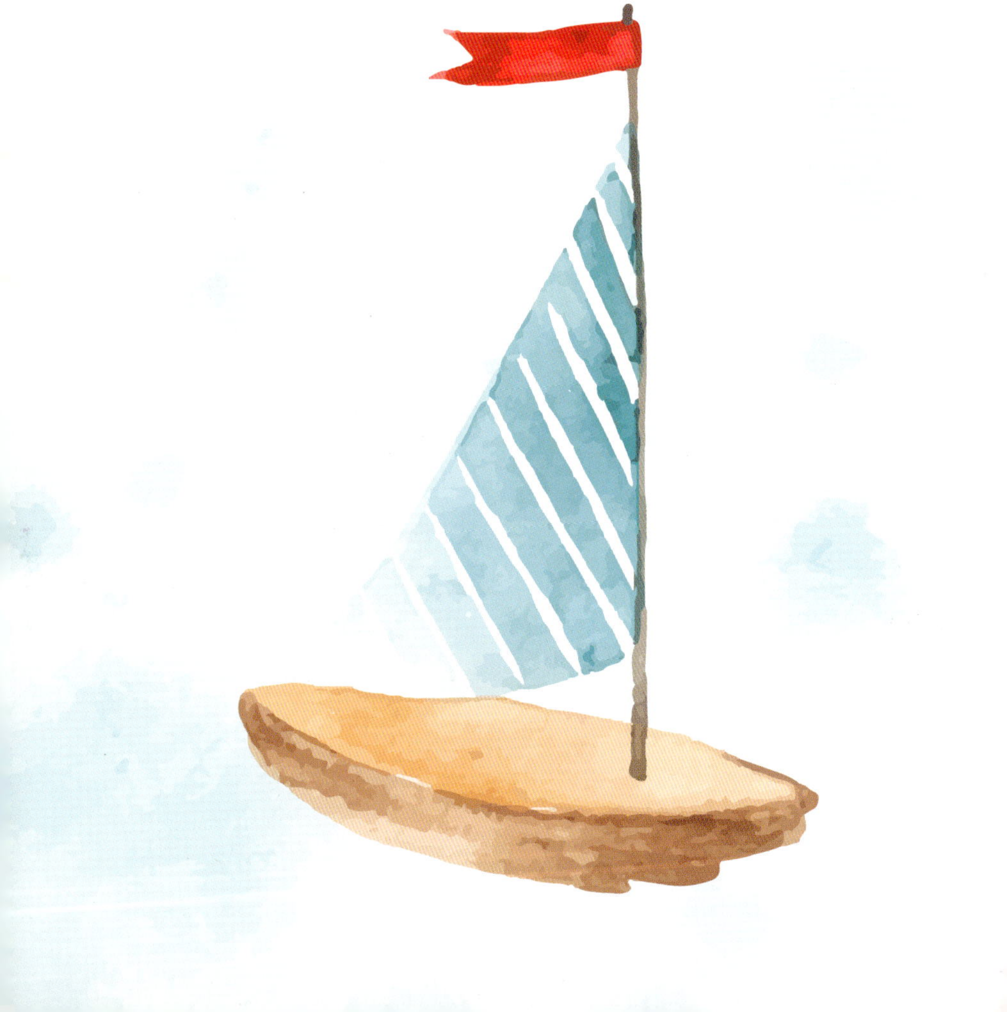

Grandpas have the patience and time to teach you how to sail a model boat or take you to a football game.

Catherine Pulsifer

You have to do your own growing no matter how tall your **grandfather** was.

Abraham Lincoln

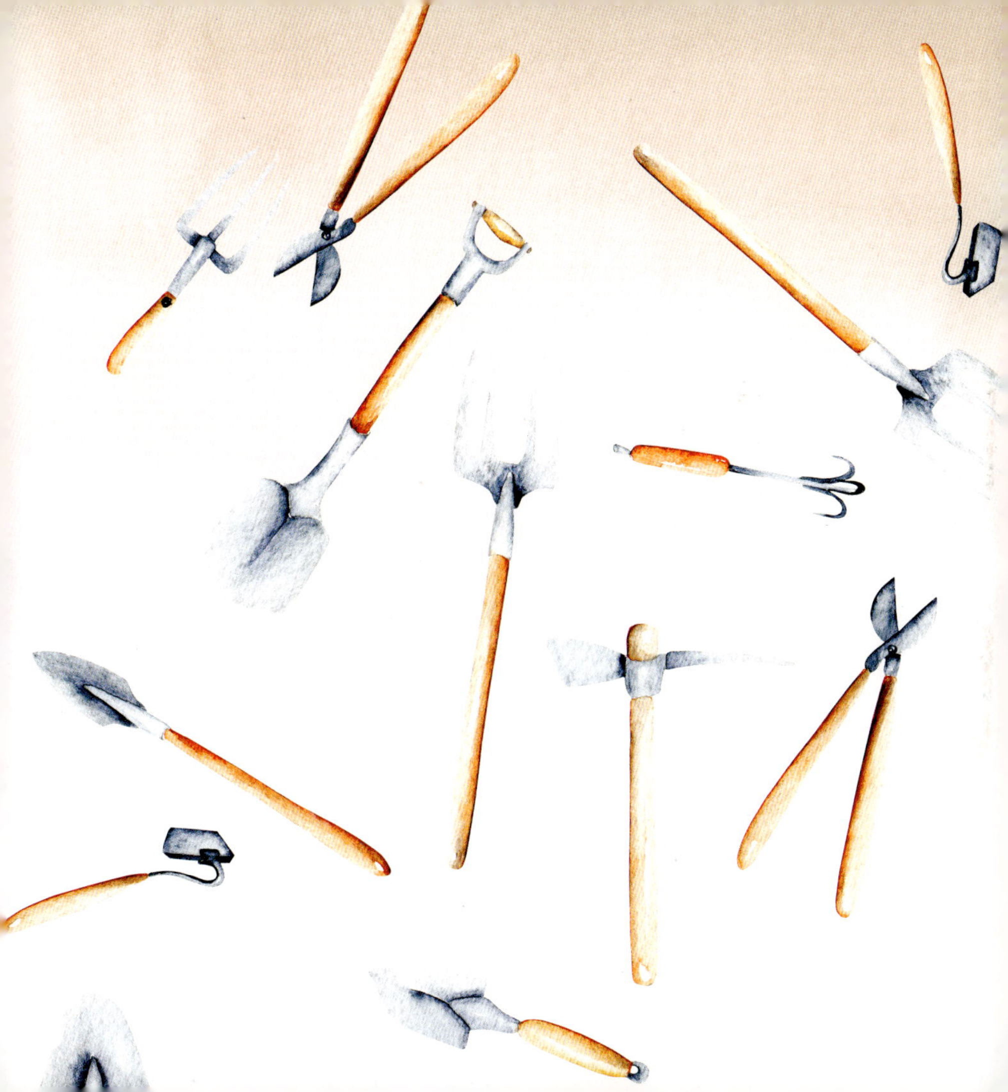

To be able to
watch your children's
children grow up . . .

. . . is truly a
blessing from above.

Byron Pulsifer

One of the most powerful handclasps
is that of a new grandbaby
around the finger of a **grandfather**.

Joy Hargrove

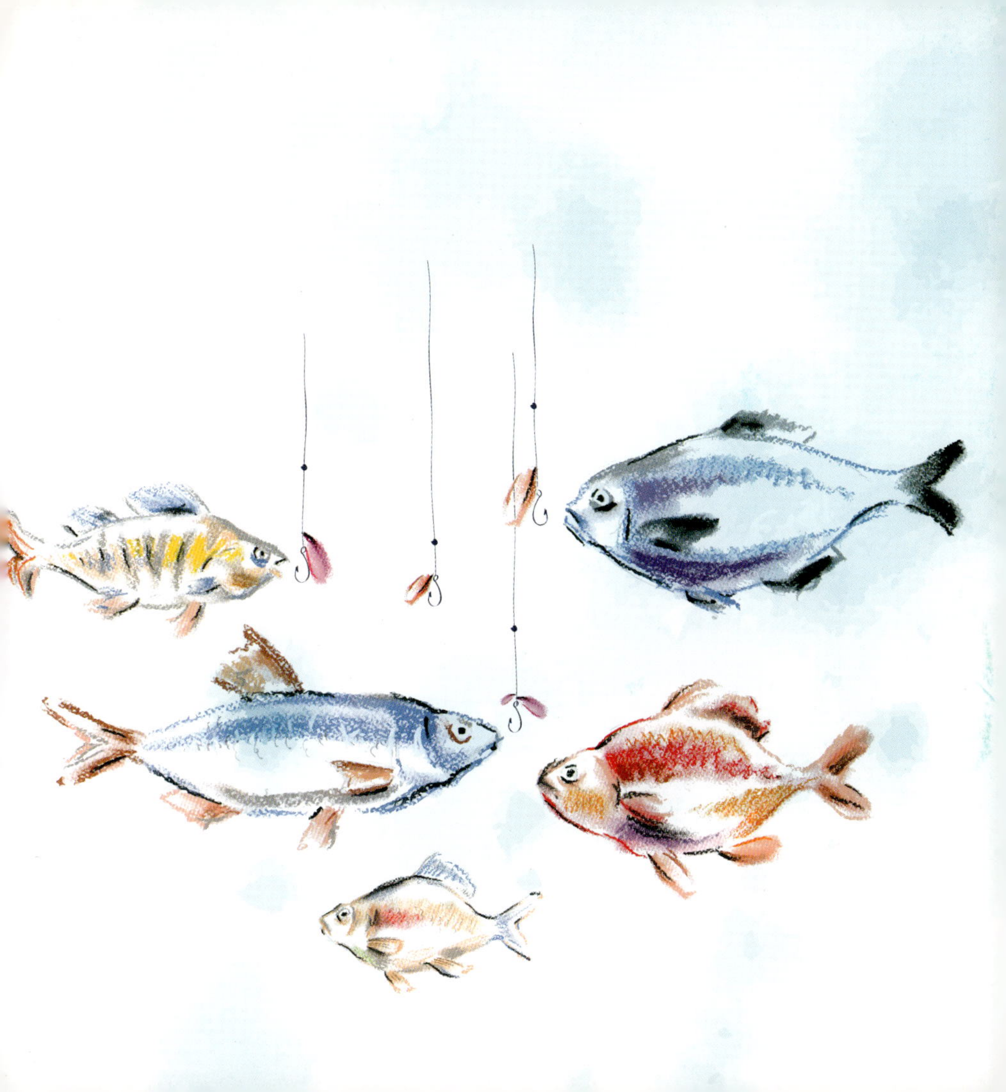

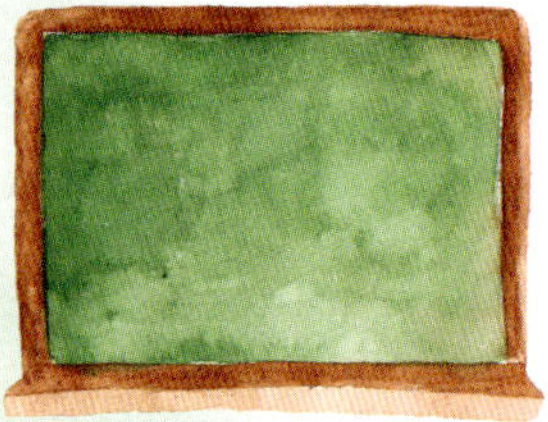
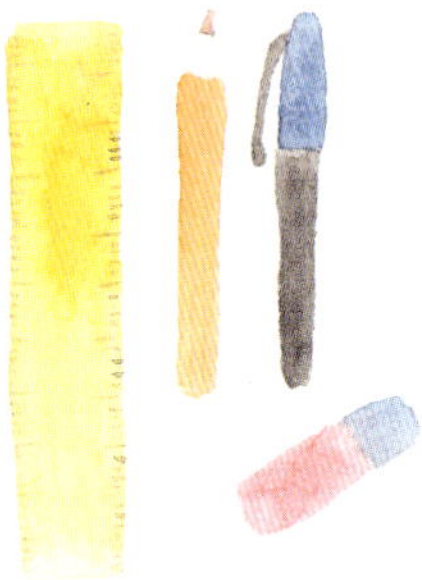
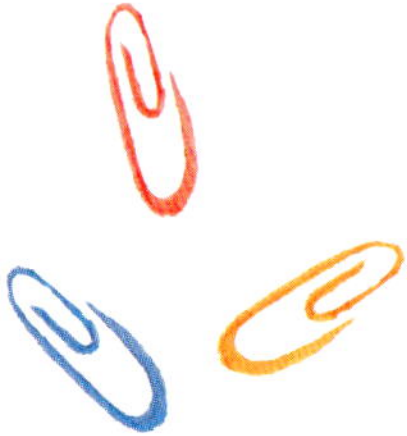
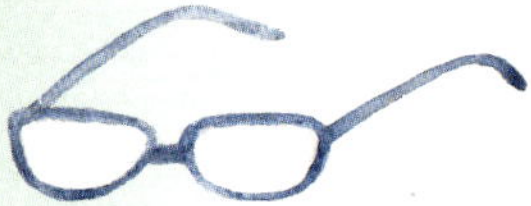
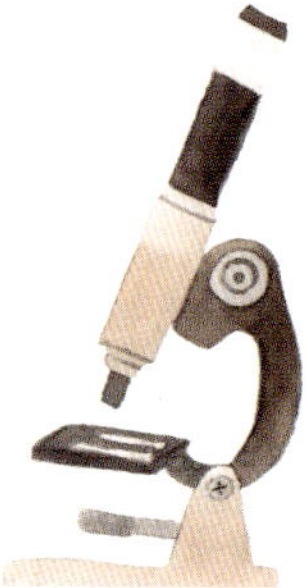
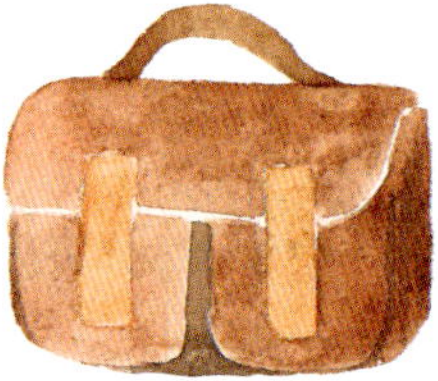
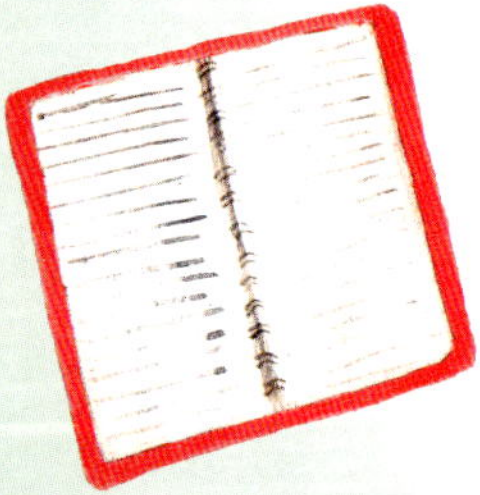

1
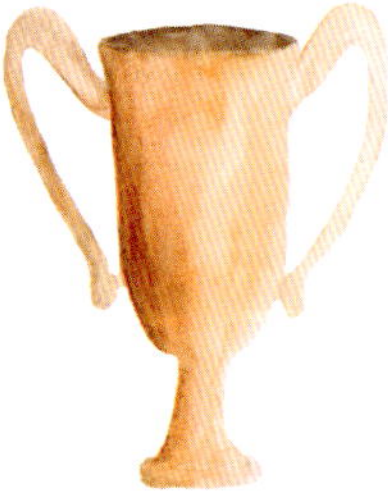

Great dads
get promoted to
grandfathers.

Author Unknown

Every generation revolts against its fathers and makes friends with its **grandfathers**.

Lewis Mumford

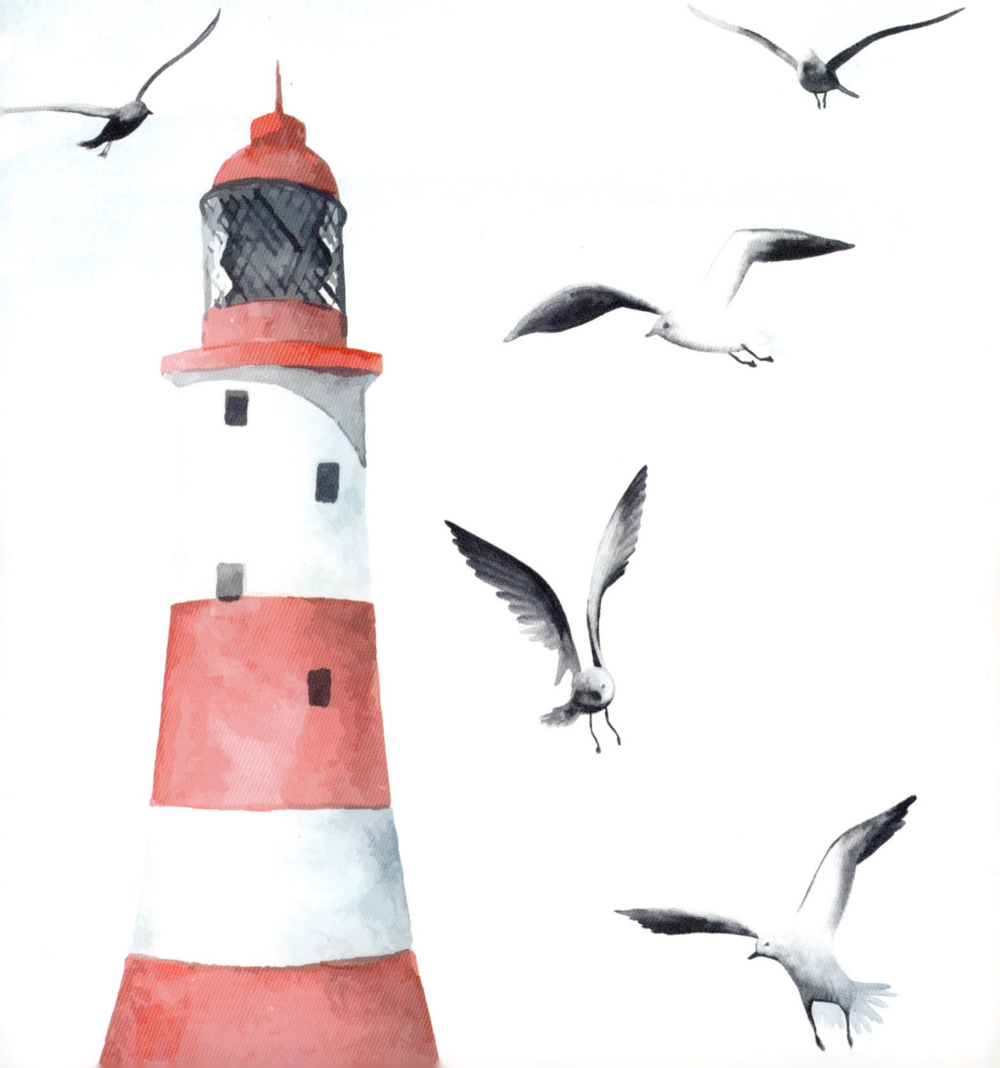

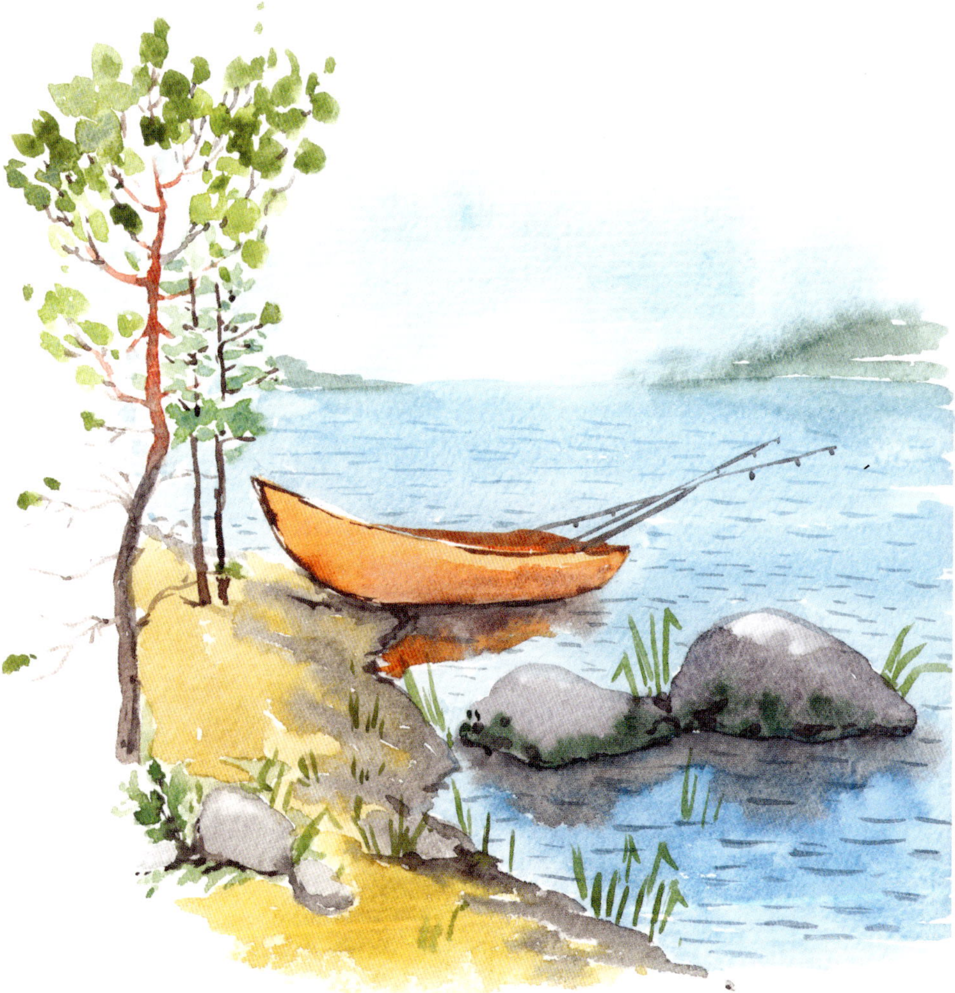

Sometimes our **grandpas** are like grand-angels.

Lexie Saige

Grandchildren don't stay young forever, which is good because **grandfathers** have only so many horsey rides in them.

Gene Perret

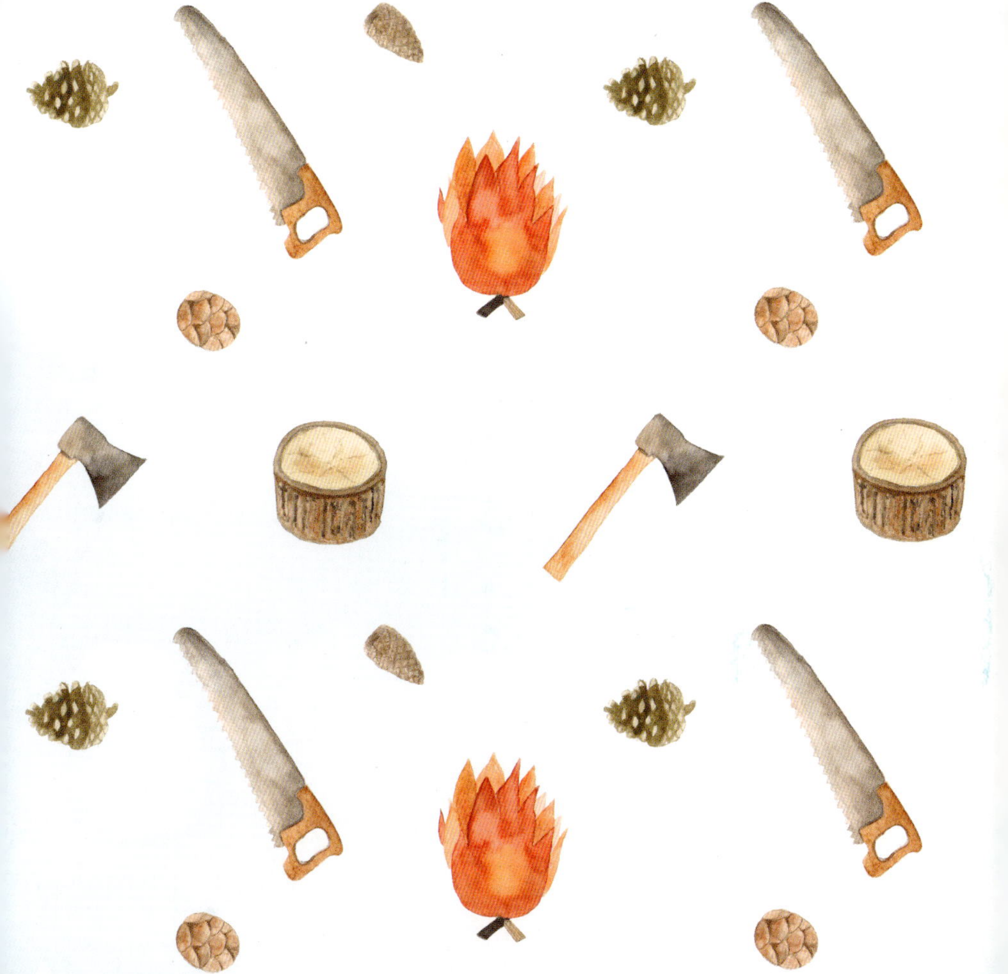

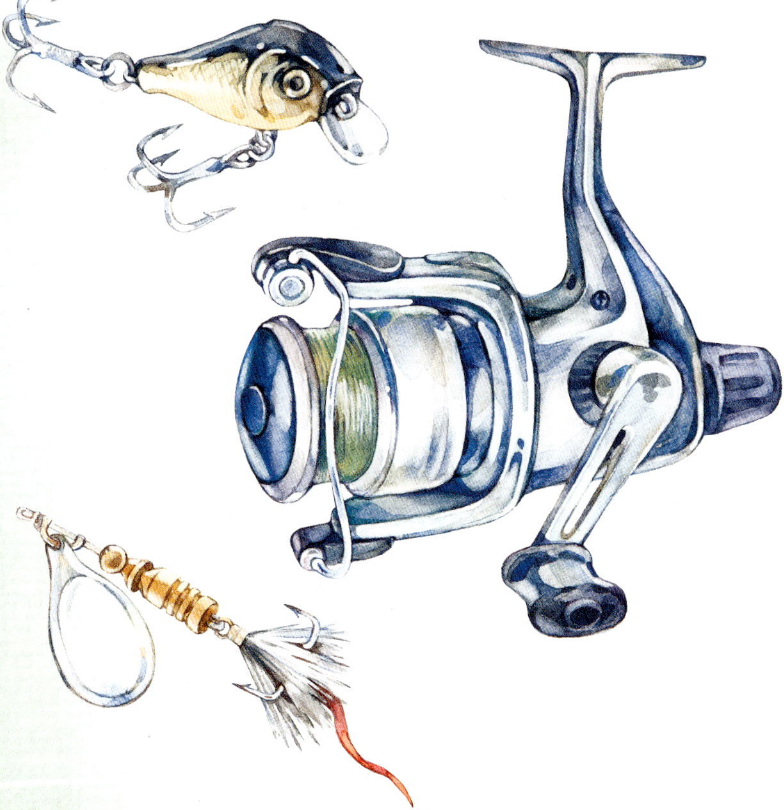

Grandfathers give us not only wisdom and encouragement, but they are an inspiration to us.

Kate Summers

My **grandfather** once told me that there are two kinds of people: those who work and those who take the credit. He told me to try to be in the first group; there was much less competition.

Indira Gandhi

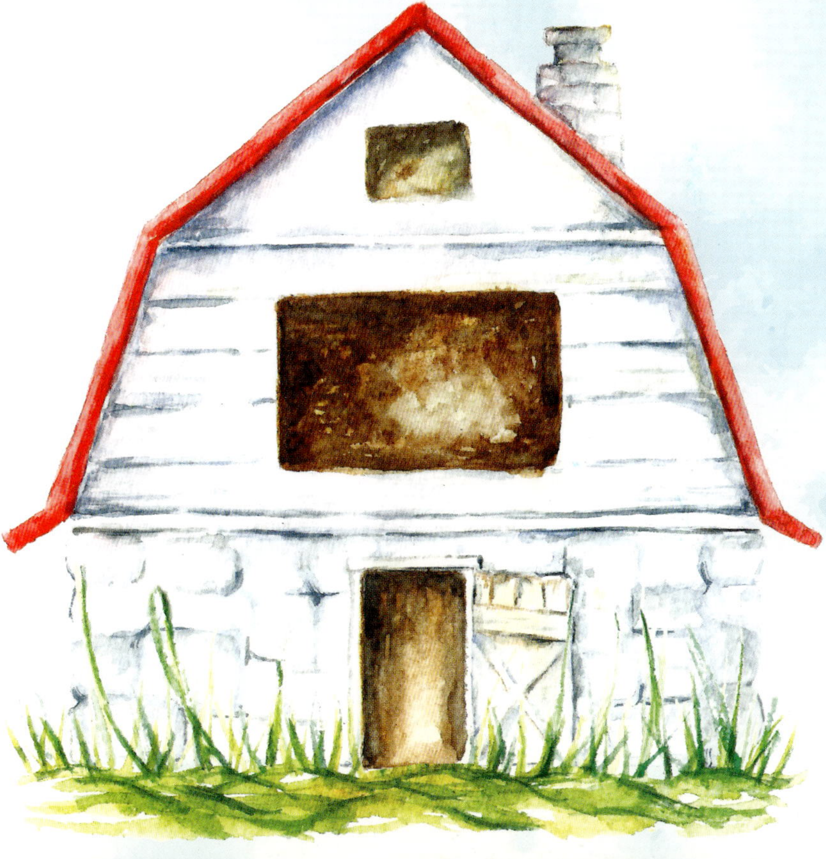

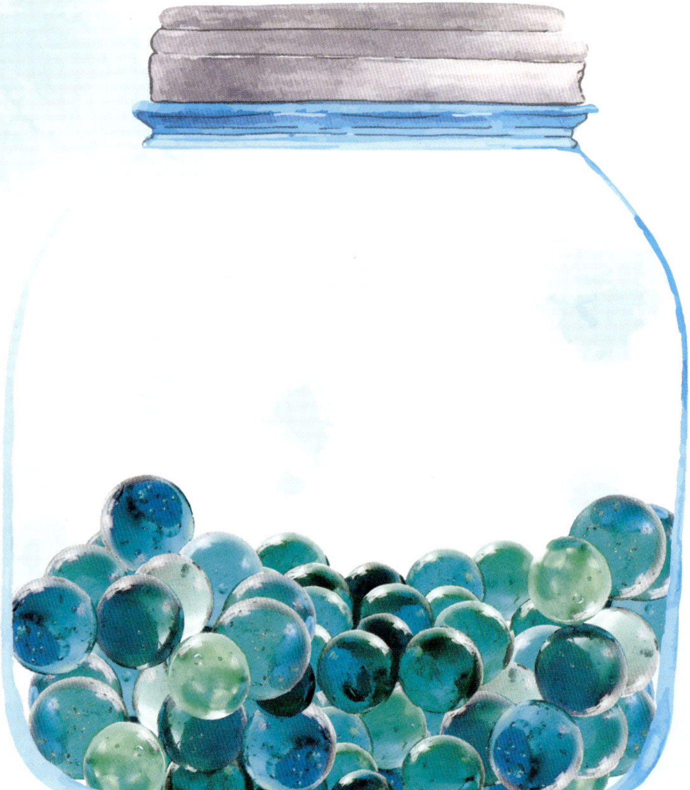

A **grandpa** is someone you never outgrow your need for.

Author Unknown

When the chips are down, grandmothers can be counted on to do whatever's necessary. When the chips are down for **grandfathers**, we just go into the kitchen and get more chips.

Michael Milligan

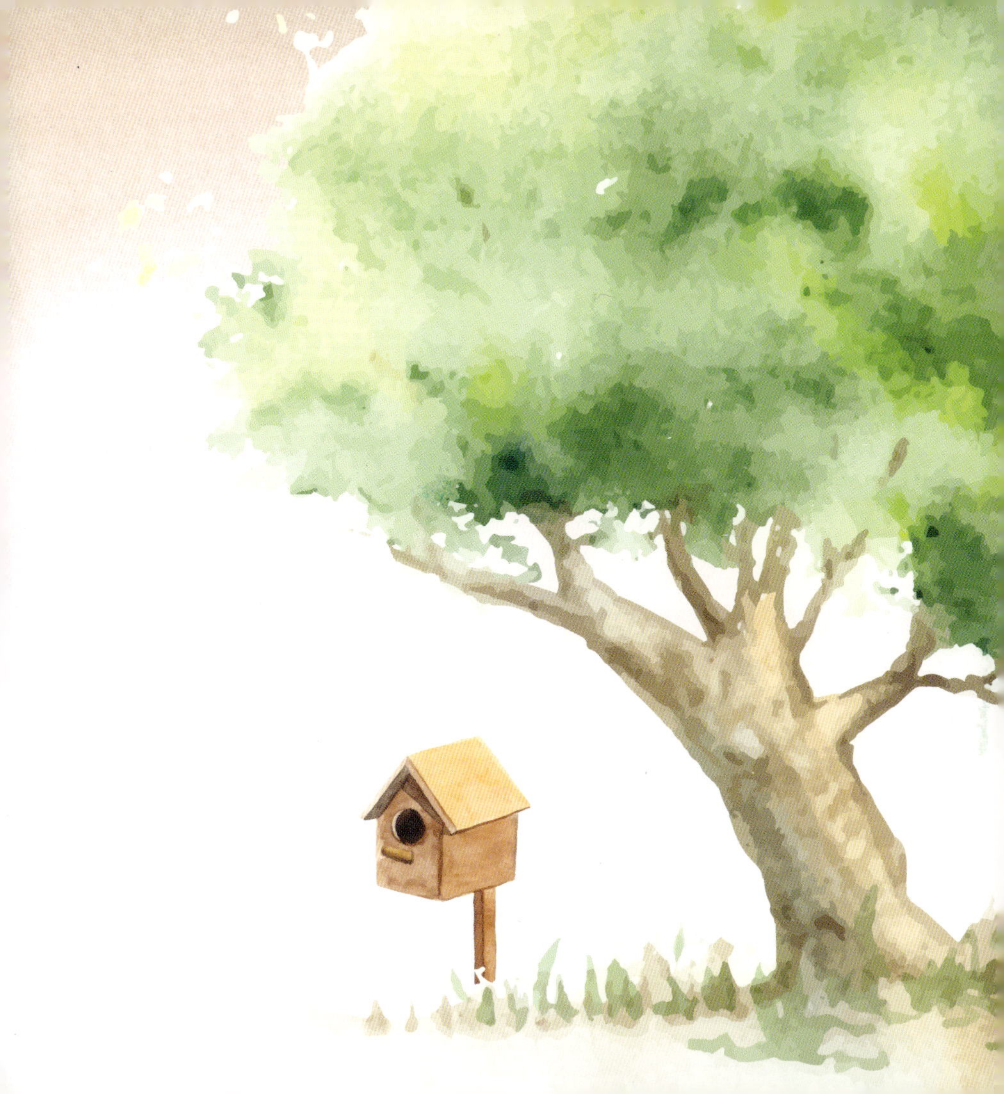

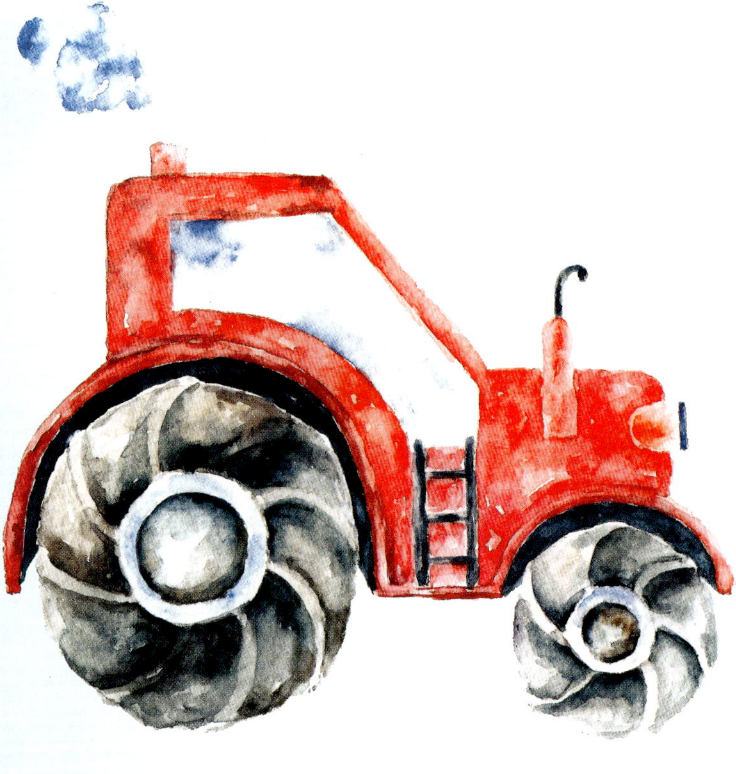

A **grandfather** makes us laugh, makes us feel safe, and always makes us feel LOVED.

Kate Summers

What children need most are the essentials that **grandparents** provide in abundance.
They give unconditional love,
kindness,
patience,
humor,
comfort,
lessons in life.
And, most importantly, cookies.

Rudolph Giuliani

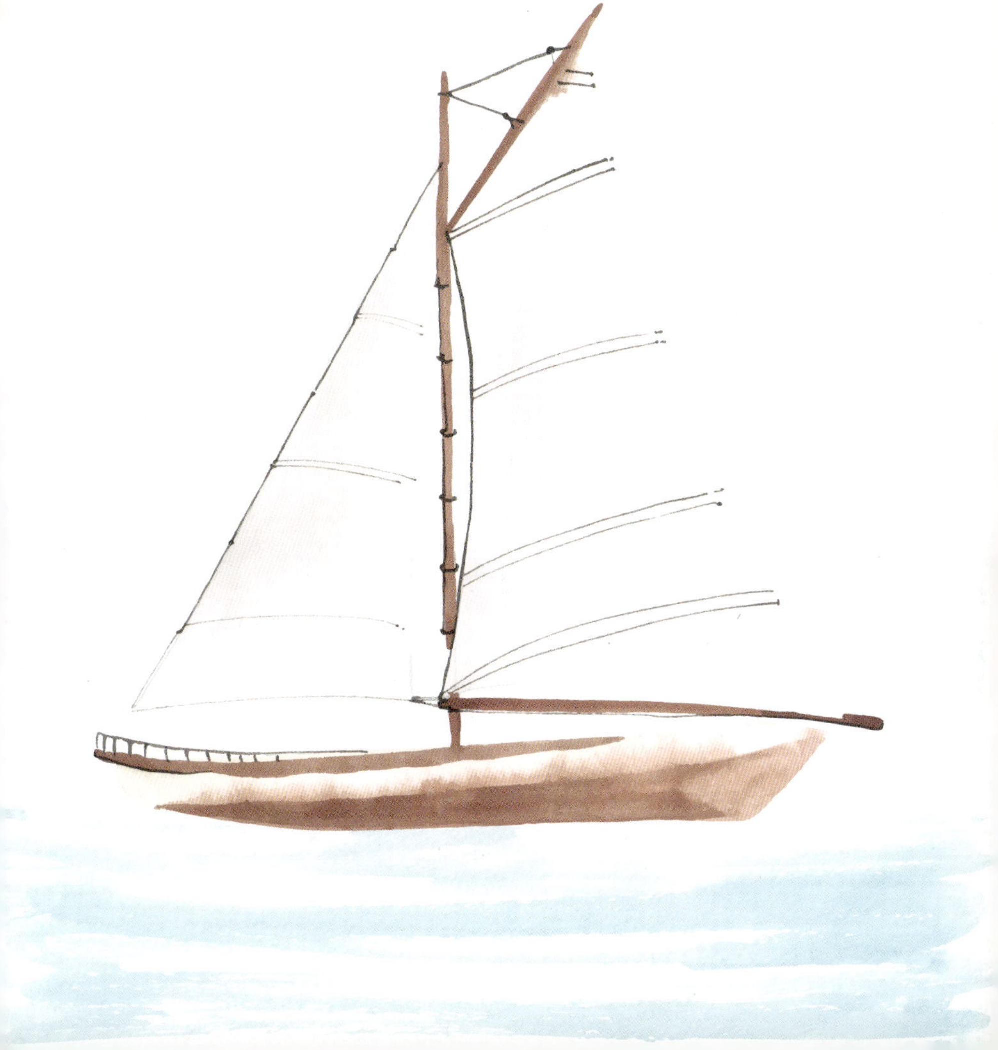

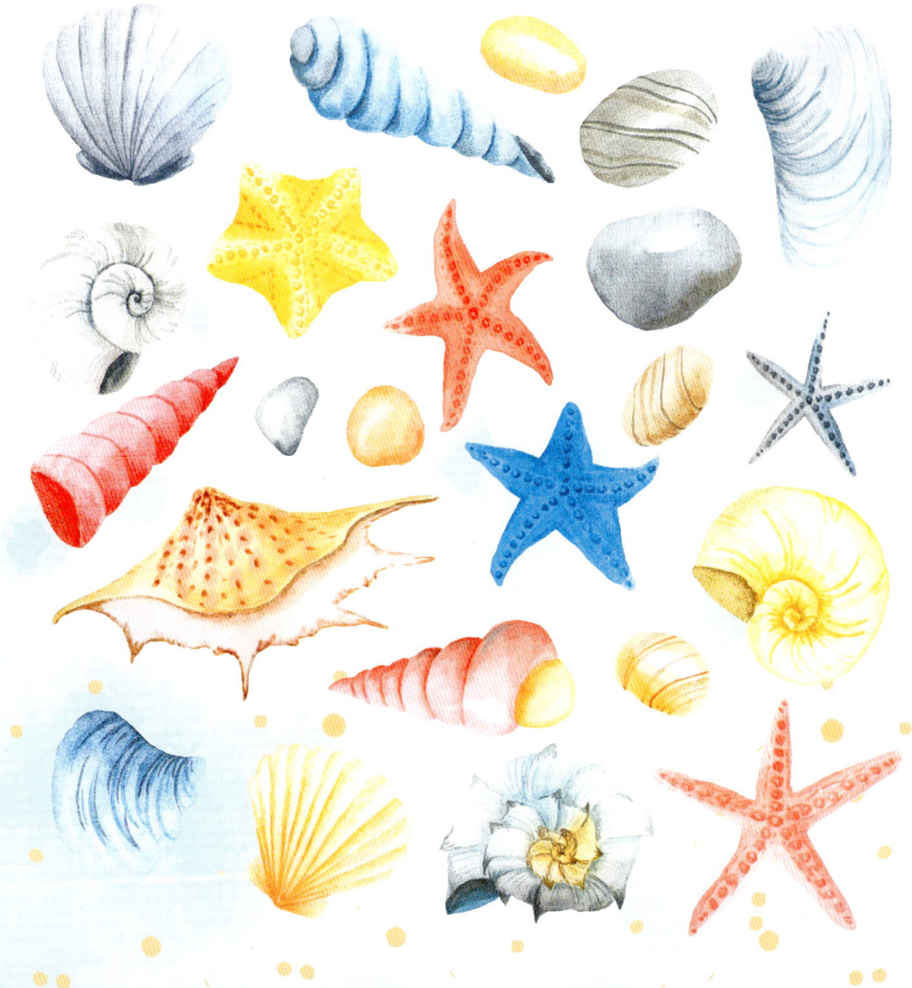

Grandpa

has ears that truly listen,
arms that always hold,
love that's never ending
and a heart that's
made of gold.

Author Unknown

The sweetest sound to the ears of a **grandfather** is the endearing name his grandchildren give him. It not only conveys recognition but also a depth of feeling expressed in no other way.

David Booth

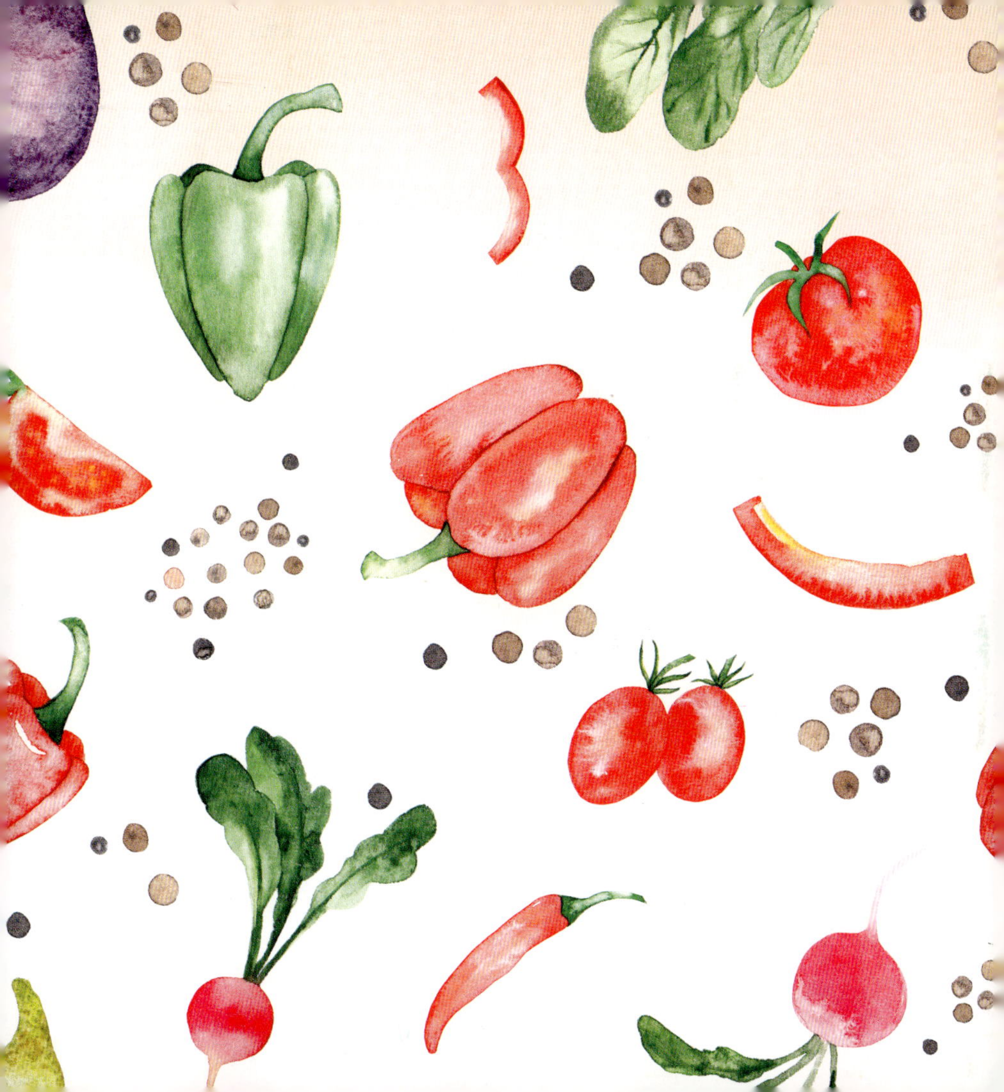

Grandpa got us up early, otherwise we might miss something.

Sunsets, he loved 'em.
Made us love 'em.

Lucille Ball

Grandfathers do have a special place in the lives of their children's children. They can delight and play with them and even indulge them in ways that they did not indulge their own children.

Alvin F. Poussaint

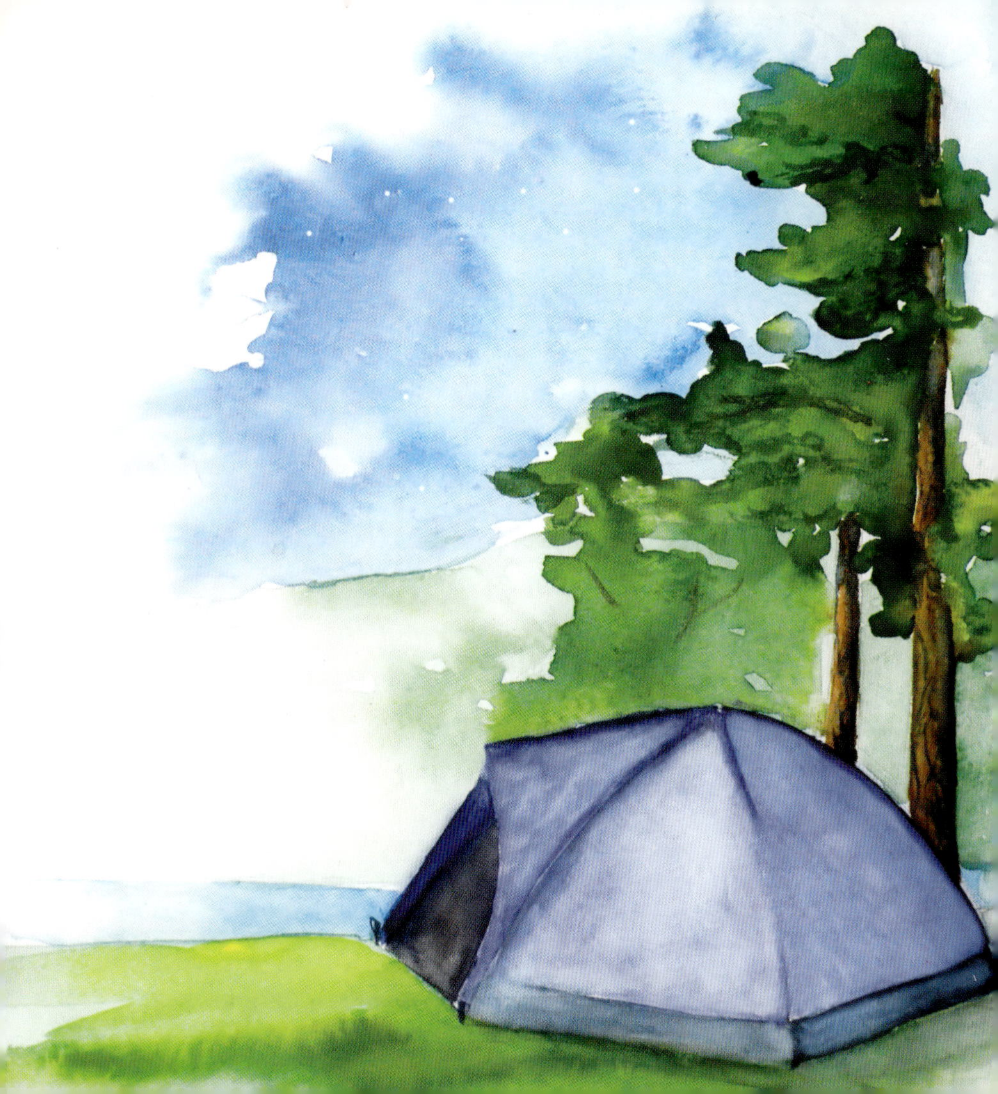

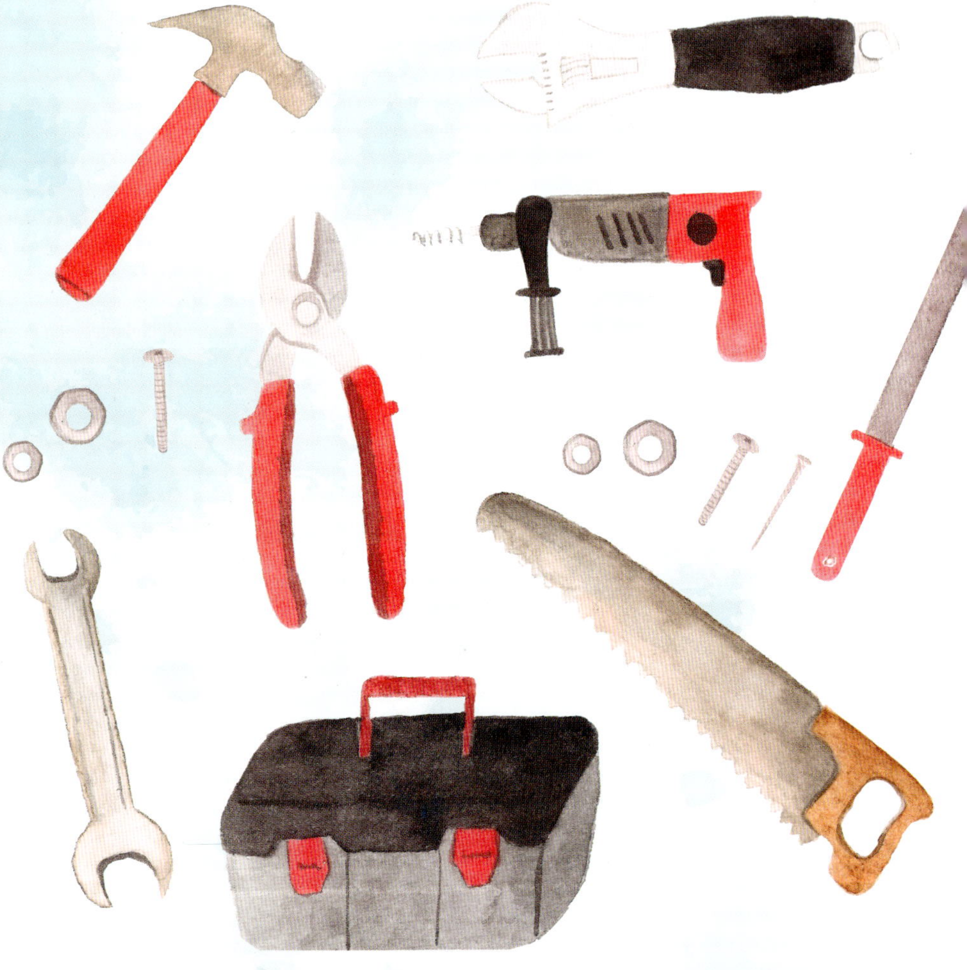

Happiness is
a **grandpa** hug.

Author Unknown

Grandfather knows that after the fun and games are over with his adorable grandchildren he can return to the quiet of his own home and peacefully reflect on this phenomenon of fatherhood.

Alvin F. Poussaint

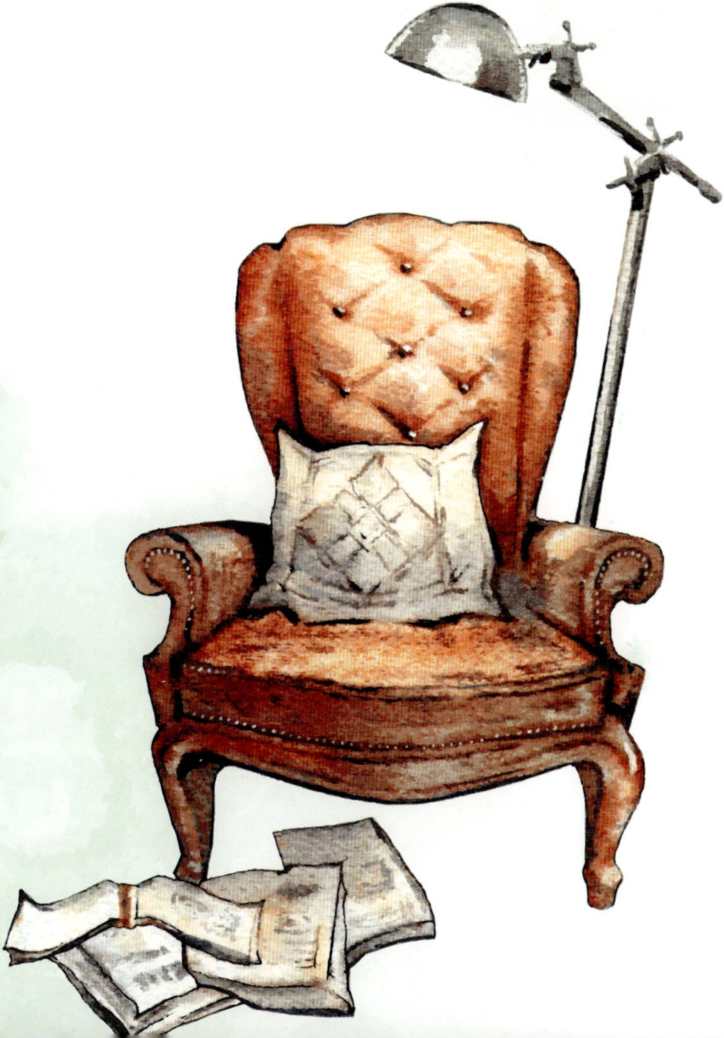

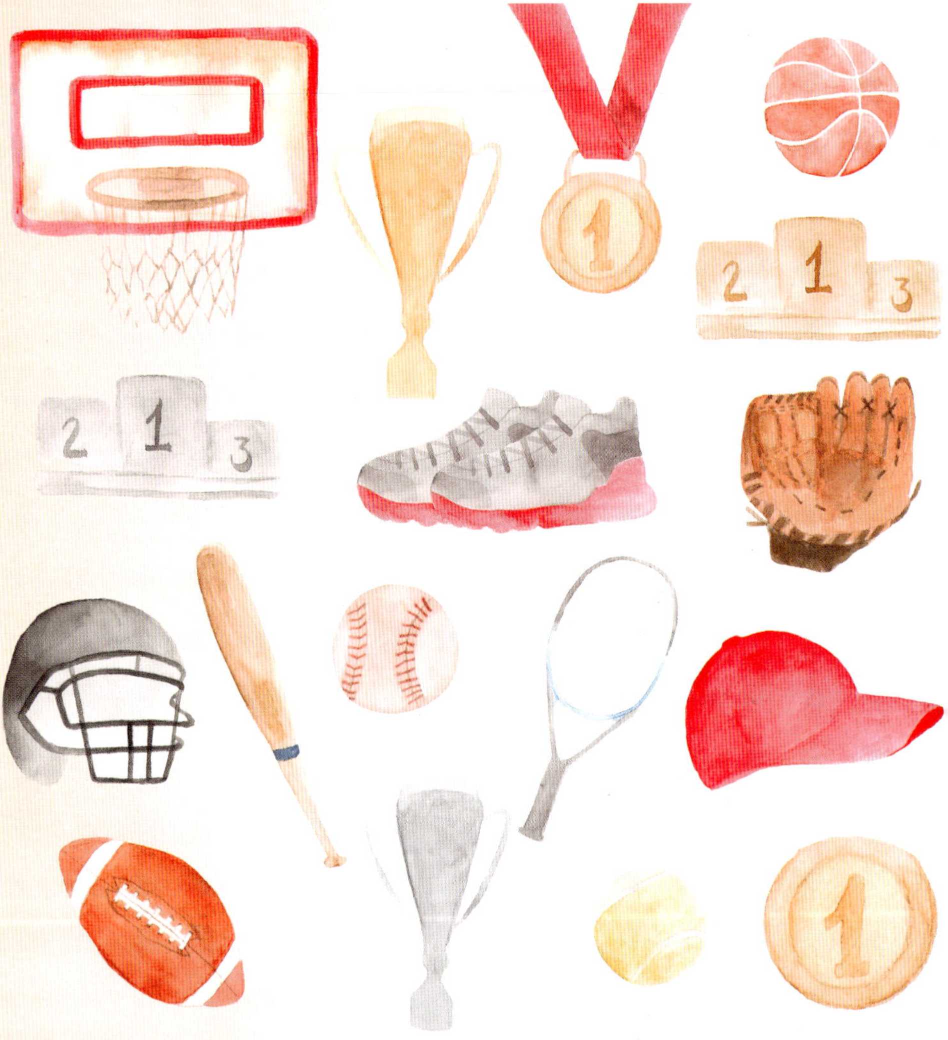
1
2 1 3
2 1 3
1

No cowboy was ever faster on the draw than a **grandfather** pulling a baby picture out of a wallet.

Author Unknown

A family with an old person has a living **treasure of gold**.

Chinese Proverb

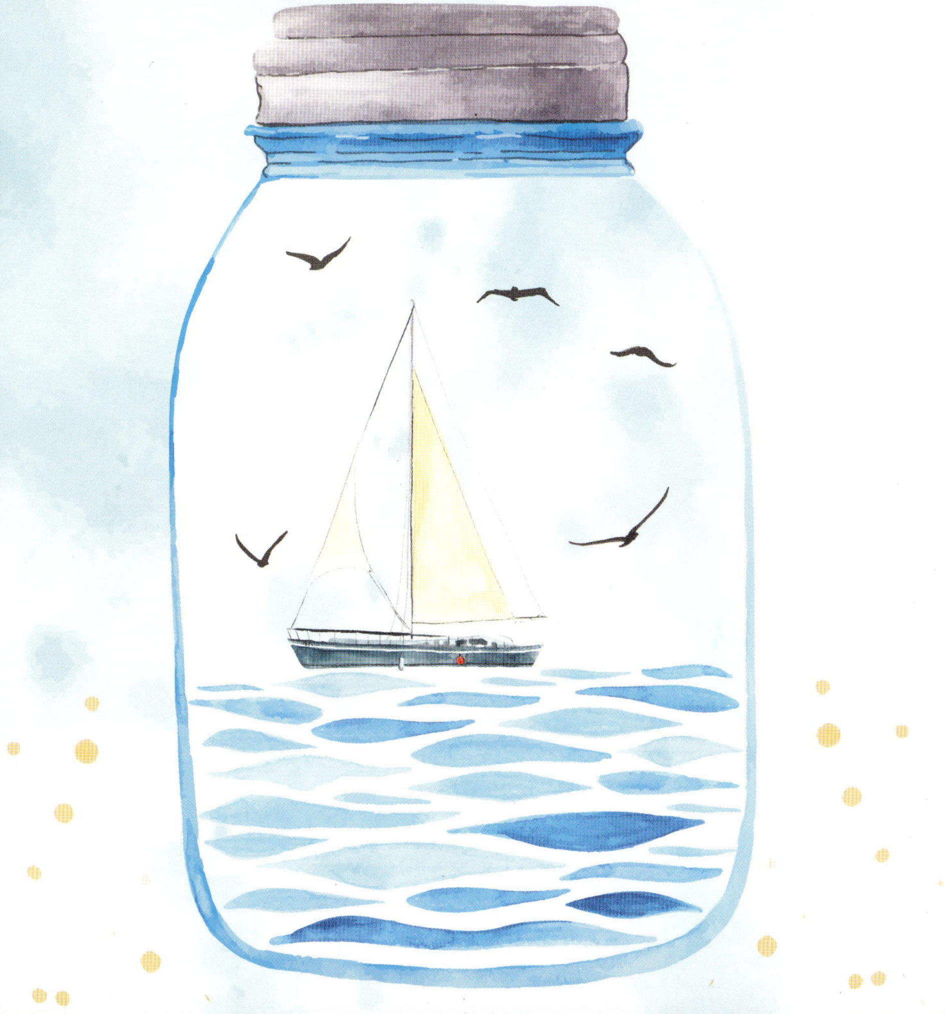

The only thing better than having you for a dad is my children having you for a **grandpa**.

Author Unknown

Image credits:
Cover & interior image credits © 2018 Bonitas/Shutterstock.com;
with the following exceptions:
pp. 10-11, 48-49 © 2018 Irina Usmanov/Shutterstock.com;
pp. 12-13 © 2018 Elyaka/Shutterstock.com;
pp. 16-17 © 2018 Catherine Glazkova/Shutterstock.com;
p. 20 © 2018 Sundra/Shutterstock.com;
p. 21 © 2018 Anastasiia Skliarova/Shutterstock.com;
pp. 22, 50-51 © 2018 helgafo/Shutterstock.com;
p. 25 © 2018 AVA Bitter/Shutterstock.com;
pp. 26, 32-33, 54, 58, 62-63 © 2018 Gulman Anya/Shutterstock.com;
p. 30 © 2018 IRINA OKSENOYD/Shutterstock.com;
p. 34 © 2018 dzujen/Shutterstock.com;
pp. 36-37, 42 © 2018 Arefyeva Victoria/Shutterstock.com;
pp. 38-39 © 2018 Andy Piatt/Shutterstock.com;
pp. 46-47 © 2018 Zabrotskaya Larysa/Shutterstock.com;
p. 52 © 2018 Maria Sem/Shutterstock.com;
p. 53 © 2018 Olga Lobareva/Shutterstock.com;
p. 57 © 2018 Penndpaper/Shutterstock.com.